POWER IN MY PAIN

The keys to convert the pain of infertility
and chronic illness into personal power

By

Danielle R. Wright

ISBN: 978-0-578-49325-1

Cover and book design by P31 Publishing.

P31 Publishing
P.O. BOX 32
LITHIA SPRINGS, GA 30122

www.wright-relations.com

❖ Dedication

To Mom and Dad - Thank you seems horribly insufficient, but it's the most complete sentence I have for all you've done for me. Your love and encouragement are undying. Your support is endless. But more importantly, your prayers covered me. Thank you for standing in the gap for me when I couldn't pray for myself.

Derrell, Kelly, Mason and Benjamin - I love you guys to the moon and beyond! Thank you for all your love and support and for taking me in when I was down and out.

Hampton Sisters, Shecoya, Monique A.J. Smith, Patricia Porter-Mayfield, Squeaky Moore, Shera White

My Squad: Andrea, Erica, Chad, Jamie (PIC), Kristen Pope, Sharaun, Taja, Tina, Toya - you guys are amazing and I can't imagine life without you!

Table of Contents

---❖---

Physical Pain

This is how it all began.

I remember being seven years old, and seeing little spots of blood on my underwear. I had really bad allergies, and, as a child, I just thought it was something normal. I was itchy all the time, I was dealing with asthma - just really severe allergies, so I didn't think anything of it. Also my mom never said anything about it, so, I figured that I was either imagining stuff, or this was just a result of an allergic reaction.

By the age of nine, my body had developed into that of a grown woman. I was wearing a C-cup bra, I had hips, thighs, gained a lot of weight, and then, *it* happened.

We were on a westward camping trip and suddenly, in the shower, blood was pouring down my legs. I thought I was going to die or something. I thought immediately, 'I need to get to the hospital'. I had no idea what was going on, but I yelled for my mom to come in and help me. That was the beginning of a painful, sometimes embarrassing, journey of reproductive illness. I had officially started my menstrual cycle at nine years old.

It took me a while to adjust to my cycle. I had to get used to charting the timing of everything - charting how things progressed with the menstrual cycle, counting 28 days, keeping a calendar, always making sure I had pads and tampons and the like. To be honest, the very first thing my mom tried at that age was a tampon and I was terrified of having anything stuck in me, especially thinking there's blood coming out of me - let's plug it up with something else. But, as time went on, I got used to it, but not really.

My period was always irregular, so charting it on a calendar or keeping track of the days in between cycles was so inconsistent and so inaccurate, that, most times, my period would just 'spring up' on me. I was always sick. I was always ill, throwing up, having severe menstrual cramps and never knew how to control it. They gave me everything from ibuprofen to prescription strength ibuprofen and other meds that did not agree with my body.

It became so bad that no medicine worked, so I just learned to deal with the menstrual cramps and take ibuprofen to take a little bit of the edge off so that I could function. I remember being in middle school, and especially in high school when it got really bad, and I would spend at least one day per month at the nurse; laid out for hours during the day, unable to walk, bleeding through my clothes, and feeling embarrassed to have to leave school or leave class to deal with my menstrual cycle. It was something that I hated, I felt embarrassed about, and not just that, but it would completely wipe me out. The physical pain was sometimes more than I thought I could bear, but, I pressed on.

By the age of 16, the menstrual cycles had become so severe that they had no choice but to put me on birth control. I remember having conversations about what birth control does and how it ultimately works to make you feel better. Unfortunately, that really didn't help either, and I was left wondering if I was always going to be in this state. Where blood was just always pouring down my legs at random moments. Where I was having to wear two sometimes three pairs of underwear, two pads, or two pads and a tampon; whatever I could get my hands on to keep the blood from soaking through my clothes.

So here I am in high school, missing days and it seemed like the only thing that was really helping monitor my bleeding was the fact that I played three sports in high school. I knew that exercise was supposed to help with painful periods, but there were some days where exercising felt like the weight of the world was on my shoulders - any movement hurt. I would wake up in the middle of the night and have to change clothes or wash up because I had bled through my pajamas, soaked through my sheets. I remember there were times where I was using towels and blankets and ultimately plastic bed covers under the sheets so that at least if I soaked through the sheets, I wouldn't mess up the mattress. That was my life. I had become used to it, I knew that every month, I was going to be in pain, I was going to have to prepare for excessive bleeding and I knew that at that point there was nothing I could do about it.

I'd been to the doctor and was told that some women just experience painful periods. That it's not as uncommon as people may think. I started my cycle early and they attributed a lot of my menstrual issues to starting at an early age, but no one really took the time to dig deeper and figure out why I was feeling the way I was feeling physically. I was physically exhausted for days, each month. As time went on through high school, and even through college, there were days where I could not get out of bed.

By the time I started college, it had progressed to the point where I was missing full days of class and work because I was bleeding so heavily. The only thing I could do was lay in bed with extra underwear on, pants, towels on the bed, and heating pads on my back and abdomen to try to relieve some of the pain and discomfort. By this time, I had stopped throwing up during my cycles, but the cramping became so severe that it caused swelling in my ankles, my calves, and my feet. Even my hands would swell up.

I had clothes just for my period. The clothes normally consisted of sweatpants, a sweatsuit of some sort, some sort of baggy t-shirt or sweatshirt because I would get so bloated that I looked pregnant; and there was nothing worse than feeling like people are looking at you as "the fat girl" or the "unwed pregnant woman." That could've been paranoia, but, to me it was *very* real. I had feelings that people were judging me based on how my body looked, not knowing what was going on internally that was causing my body to change. I felt like I was going through a metamorphosis every month where I would change into a "beluga whale" and would be so swollen that I literally had a separate wardrobe just for my cycle.

Aside from needing a separate wardrobe, I also knew that there were some dietary changes I needed to make and I needed to work out more. When I was in college, I went through the whole gaining the "Freshman 15", 20, 30 pounds, but I was also dealing with the realization that my menstrual cycle continued to spiral downward and completely out of control. It was something that had consumed me. I planned outfits, events, and trips around my period. It was something that I, at the time, didn't realize was impacting me mentally, spiritually, and emotionally.

I continued to change my diet, I continued to exercise as allowed, clearly not as much as I should have. Definitely not as much as I should have. But I remained active, remained active in extracurricular activities, and tried my hardest to not allow my reproductive system to completely overwhelm my life - but that proved to be more difficult as time went on. No amount of diet and exercise was helping me maintain or contain my weight. I 'blew up'. As I started graduate school, I realized I was at my heaviest weight ever, but there was more.

The diet and exercise were often overridden by sleep deprivation. If you can imagine not being able to sleep because you're waking up multiple times in the middle of the night to go to the bathroom, to change your clothes because you feel wet, because you have bled through something, or because you're afraid to bleed through and mess up sheets and towels. All that causes a lack of sleep. Not to mention the severe pain. The physical pain was unrelenting. I was cramping in the middle of the night, and my calves would turn into rocks because my menstrual cramps are so bad that I had pain shooting from my abdomen down through my hips and legs, into my feet at times. It was excruciating, but moreover, it was exhausting.

I remember trying to find more natural ways to get rest at night, so I was taking ibuprofen to help thin the blood out, I was also taking melatonin and some natural supplements to help me relax and rest at night. But nothing seemed to work. I was still absolutely exhausted. During grad school, I made sure I not only had one or two changes of clothes with me, but I always carried kind of an overnight bag of stuff - from baby wipes to a full pack of overnight menstrual pads, to ibuprofen. Basically everything I would need for an accident. Knowing that at any moment there could be an accident; but I was sleep deprived.

Somehow I made it through grad school, but the pain that ensued during grad school was unbearable. One night, I was coming home from class, I had gone to the grocery store, and made my way home. I got into the house, and immediately felt the most intense, and excruciating pain I had ever felt in my entire life.

This excruciating pain lasted for months. I never knew what was going on. I couldn't figure it out. But, I knew that it was intensifying each month. Of course, having an irregular menstrual cycle, I was always attributing it to my menstrual cycle and nothing else. Whether there was blood or not, I always assumed that at any time, my period would just start and be ruthless, unrelenting and pop up unannounced because that's typically what would happen.

In 2006, during grad school, I met up with my dad at a regional NCAA basketball tournament game. We caught two games that night and as we were leaving the arena, I remember doubling over. I had a pain that not only stopped me dead in my tracks from walking, but I wasn't sure that I could take another step forward.

I told my parents about the pain I was experiencing. I had been to the gynecologist a few times and they just couldn't figure it out. Again, given my menstrual cycle and reproductive health history, the doctor attributed it to dysmenorrhea which is basically a medical term for heavy or irregular bleeding. Doesn't help much when you have excruciating pain that comes and goes unannounced.

So, we stopped, I'm doubled over, I'm crying, and I just remember thinking, God, this feels like someone is taking a hammer and nail to my insides, for lack of a better analogy. Not to be too vulgar, but, if you can imagine your flesh being torn, or you have a severe injury that involves the tearing of your flesh, that's pretty much what was happening to my insides. That was in March of 2006.

The next week, I scheduled an appointment and I had an ultrasound and an MRI, and other testing done. I had to go in, during my period, I had a pelvic exam and I remember thinking, I'm in enough pain as it is with my period, and now you're sticking things in me, twisting things around, sticking me with needles to draw blood, I'm done. I was exhausted. As I stated before, my period was something that absolutely drained me. And so having to do a pelvic exam while I was on my period added to not just the discomfort, but the pain afterward, because the cramping would get worse. Everytime I had a pelvic exam, I would cramp for days afterward. It was like my body was saying, "I literally hate you, and I'm going to cause you even more pain because you're trying to figure out what's going on and sticking foreign objects in me to figure it out. I'm gonna make you pay for it," and my body did just that.

After about four days or so, the doctor called me back and said, "we need to do exploratory surgery because you have all the signs and symptoms of endometriosis." I had no idea what they were talking about. I asked them to spell it, type it out, send me an email and articles on it, because I had absolutely no idea what endometriosis was. I needed help.

Of course, I was in grad school, so the first thing I did was begin to research it on my own. I was slated for surgery the first week of

April 2006, my parents came out for the operation and the end result was them telling me that I had endometriosis. For those of you that don't know, endometriosis is when the lining of the uterus grows outside of the uterus and so it's almost like having extra endometrial tissue attaching to other organs and other tissue in your pelvic area.

In my case, it was causing a lot of pain because it was attaching to the back or behind the uterus, and also downward towards my anus. Now all of the issues and pain made sense. My uterus was actually tilted backward, so it was at a slant. And, not realizing this, the doctor told me that a tilted uterus alone is painful and can cause painful periods. So I was getting a double dose. I was not really prepared for what they were telling me next, "we don't know why it happens and there is no cure for it. But we know that surgery and birth control help." So I said, ok great, let's get back on birth control and go from there.

Surgery was successful, and they removed all endometriosis that they found during the operation, and I was on the road to recovery, or so I thought. I say, "or so I thought" because, I never realized that the road to recovery was going to be unending. What came next were years of pain, heavy bleeding, and not knowing how to control everything that was going on with my body.

In 2008, I was faced with another operation. After a couple of months of being home, I was forced into the same procedure that led to my diagnosis in 2006. So, to the operating table,

I went again. Afterward, I was placed on birth control, again. But what happened next was something that would terrify anyone, especially any woman. Birth control caused me to bleed out of control. I went back to the doctor after two weeks and told them, "I have not stopped bleeding." The doctor told me to keep taking the pills because my body just needed time to adjust. And sometimes after surgery, your hormones are out of balance and then you're trying to add hormones back in to stabilize everything. But, the bleeding never stopped.

A month later, I went back and I told him that he had to find something else to give me because I was still bleeding. He told me that everything was "normal" and that there's really nothing wrong. That, the bleeding I was experiencing is simply my body trying to adjust to birth control. By this time it was March. I was nearly three months post op, and still bleeding. It was another three months of bleeding with only a few days in between my cycle while I was on birth control. I suddenly was feeling the affects of it. Over time I had become so fatigued that I was showing up late to work. I was, again, sleep deprived. I made another appointment, and he told me I could come off birth control "if I wanted to," but he doesn't suggest it.

After six months, I was feeling completely dejected and feeling like I did not know my own body. Afterall, my own gynecologist, a medical professional, telling me that what I was experiencing was normal. By this point, I had equated my entire life to that of "the woman with the issue of blood" in the Bible who bled uncontrollably for 12 years with no relief (Mark 5:25-34). Her story, her life, had become mine. And all I could think was to cry out to God for help. But even in that, I was wondering if God truly heard my cries. Could he really hear me? And if he could, why was He allowing a doctor, a medical professional, to continue having me go through what I was experiencing. Why would he allow a medical professional to not believe me? This was my body. I needed him to believe me.

In June 2008 I was facing another issue; fatigued, tired, sleep deprived, and obviously lacking some key nutrients because I had lost so much blood over the last, now, almost seven months, I was forced to make a decision for myself. I remember being at work and having to leave because I was so sick. I couldn't stand, I could not focus, I was completely tired, and at that point had actually had to go to the bathroom during my lunch break, change my clothes to freshen up a bit because I had bled through my work clothes.

One of my friends from work called her mom and asked her mom to help us. Her mom got online and found a doctor for me in the Cleveland area. We were looking at specialists for endometriosis. I never knew these specialists existed. My gynecologist at the time never told me that these specialists existed. It's frightening what you don't know, until you realize you don't know it. You find out information that you should have known years ago, that a medical professional probably should have referred you to someone with a little more experience or a little more focused training in a specific area.

I knew there were oncologists for people who had medical issues with cancer or precancer. I knew that there were endocrinologists for people with diabetes and other endocrinological health issues. I never knew that there gynecologists who specialize in endometriosis.

I was able to get an appointment with a specialist at the Cleveland Clinic in July 2008. By the time I went to see her, my condition had worsened to the point where the lining of my uterus was so thin that it was literally "oozing." It was bleeding out of control and was like I had holes in the lining of my uterus. I never knew that birth control could do that to my body or be a contributing factor. I always looked at it as something that would help me, not hurt me even worse - but there's more.

After months of drinking sugary, electrolyte-filled drinks like Gatorade and ginger ale, and things to supplement the nutrients I was losing, I was diagnosed with type 2 diabetes. Now, I have a family history of diabetes, plus with my weight issues, something in the back of my mind told me it was a possibility. But still, I just didn't think it would happen this way. In fact, I kind of thought that everything I was experiencing was due to the amount of blood I was losing.

After several tests, diabetes was confirmed. But it was also con-firmed that I had endometriosis again. Months after this opera-tion, it had returned, and I was experiencing the pain and bleed-ing in a way that seemed to be unbearable and completely out of control. So the doctor suggested that I not use any hormonal supplements. No more birth control, no more progesterone or anything like that. I was strictly going to let my body heal.

But the healing never really came. Although, my uterine lining returned to a normal thickness, the pain never went away. The heavy periods never subsided and I was left, again, planning out vacations, planning out trips, planning out my work day, all around my menstrual cycle. All I could think when I left in the morning was "make sure you have plenty of adult diapers and overnight pads, never run out of baby wipes, always keep an extra pair of underwear with you, and always make sure you have two changes of clothes."

That was my life. I was literally living the life of "the woman with the issue of blood" knowing there were times where if I went out in public, I might have to deal with the embarrassment of having blood on my sweater, on my pants, on my shirt, or sometimes on the lining of my socks at the end of the day because blood had dripped down my leg.

I continued to see the specialist and she monitored my progress and monitored how I was feeling. She kept me off of birth con-trol but told me to make sure that I was taking Ibuprofen. By

September of 2008, something went terribly wrong. I remember waking up and feeling as though I had been set on fire. Keep in mind, I was still bleeding. After eight or nine months straight of wearing a pad and tampons, my reproductive system seemed to be in disarray, more than ever.

I remember being diligent about checking myself, about looking at my vaginal area and making sure that there was nothing too out of the norm. Mostly because the original gynecologist that I saw when I moved back to Ohio really didn't believe anything that I was experiencing. So I began to take pictures and tried to document everything that I saw, or experienced so that someone would believe me.

I woke up one morning and felt again as if everything was on fire. I grabbed a mirror and noticed that all of my skin around my vulva and my anus was raw. I had cuts, I had raw flesh showing. It was red. It was thickened in certain areas and it was severely inflamed. Above all else, my skin had turned completely white. I wasn't sure what this was from, but I was petrified. All I could think was "is this what diaper rash is?" From my experience with babies, I've seen diaper rash, and this kind of looked like it, and it made sense since I was wearing a pad for eight months straight.

But nonetheless, at my next check-up with Dr. M., she looked at it and said "we need to test this. It looks like it could be more than just an infection." Hearing that you never know what that means, but, she did the biopsy and during that time I was awake. I remember her numbing the area a little bit, and then clipping some of the tissue. She also did a cervical scrape and a vaginal scrape to test the cells in those two areas. What came back was alarming and something else I was just not prepared for. It was about two weeks later and I was at work. The Cleveland Clinic has this awesome system where all of your patient information gets uploaded electronically, you get your test results, lab results, and everything else online. I remember getting an email saying that I had new information that was uploaded to my patient portal. So, I logged in during my lunch break and saw the diagnosis: "Vin IV." I had absolutely no idea what "Vin IV" was, so immediately, I did a Google search for it to see what kind of medical terminology it was. The results results came back as precancer, stage 4. Now, I had no idea what that was. Of course I had saw the word "cancer" and I had freaked out assuming that this diagnosis was going to turn into cancer. I went into my dad's office, he was one of my direct bosses, and burst into tears. I sobbed uncontrollably and told him what the results were. So, in his office, I'm fearful, scared, nervous, upset, crying, and in true "Dad fashion," he was able to calm me down enough to talk me through with spiritual guidance using scriptures. He also talked about his own health journey.

I went back to my desk, finished my work day, and called the nurse to make sure that I understood the results. So, after work, I received a return phone call from the nurse who confirmed that this is what they call Stage IV Vin and I asked for a deeper explanation as to what that was, what it meant, and what was next.

In our conversation she explained that precancer cells are the process of cells beginning to mutate and become abnormal. It was not cancer yet, but left uncontrolled, it could turn into cancer. Abnormal cells, known as dysplasia, were on my cervix. I also had some in the vaginal canal, but most of the cells were on the vulva. It had spread so far around the vulva, that they were looking at doing a biopsy in three or four different areas. I was immediately referred to one of the oncologists at the Cleveland Clinic who called me in for an appointment and biopsy next week. Again, all I could think was "more pain." I'm tired of being poked and prodded, pricked, blood drawn, solutions poured on my body in different areas to test this, that, and the third. I really just wanted to be done. But my journey was not over.

I went in to see the doctor who confirmed the diagnosis and also told me that I needed surgery. I thought that I could wait. He said that the condition was pretty severe and was going to require an extensive operation. In my head, I'm thinking, "what is an 'extensive operation'? Could it possibly be any worse than what I already had?" I explained to him that I really didn't want surgery and that I needed to know all of the details on what to expect because my last gynecologist was not forthcoming with the information that I needed and the post operation experience was horrible and frightening at times. So he sat down with me and went through everything. He told me what to expect, and also told me that my recovery time due to the extent of the treatment was going to be a month. I had never in my life taken off a month of anything, not school, not work, nothing. So being home for a full month was a bit frightening for me as well. I was scared about losing my job, I was scared about not being able to do the things that I love to do.

At this point, I was really feeling this was kind of the fault of my previous gynecologist. I felt like, he should have believed me and maybe if he believed me he would've been able to do something more or I could have somehow gotten to see Dr. M. prior to seven months of bleeding. But here we were- I was sitting here in a doctor's office facing my second operation in 10 months.

October came and it was time for the surgery. After a couple of hours, they had completely lasered the entire vulvar area. They burned away all the cells and told me that I was basically left with second degree burns in that area. If you can imagine the pain of being burned when you maybe nicked your hand or arm taking something out of the oven, and intensify that, that was my entire vaginal area.

The recovery process was slow, painful, frustrating, but somehow through God's grace, I made it through. It wasn't always easy, there were times where I really wanted to throw in the towel and say enough is enough, but I knew that the last thing I wanted was cancer. I knew that the last thing I wanted was a result that was even worse than what I had. I asked the doctor how this could happen? How could I have gotten to this stage so quickly? He said there were signs before, there were probably symptoms before, but the symptoms mimic that of a yeast infection. And then I stopped. I was disappointed and angry with myself because I always thought I just had a serious issue with yeast infections so I always spent time making sure that my reproductive hygiene was on point. And then when I was diagnosed with diabetes earlier in '08, before this operation, I was told that diabetics are more susceptible to infections and women are highly susceptible to yeast infections. So for me, that was my answer. I was getting yeast infections because I was diabetic and for months had no idea. In actuality, it was not due to diabetes. It was due to the fact that I had precancerous cells that had spread and were mimicking symptoms of a yeast infection. The itching, the burning, the inflamation, sometimes even the odor were all because of this pre-cancer condition.

I felt like I should've been relieved, but in the back of my mind, I just kept thinking about all the "what ifs" and what's next. I was told that I would always be high risk for reproductive cancers. That's not exactly what you want to hear. And I understand that it's the doctor's job to be forthcoming with all information as much as possible and as soon as possible, however, I was not prepared for that bit of information. I was not prepared to hear that my reproduction was in jeopardy. Over what? I couldn't even fathom being told that something I had no control over could cause me to be infertile. But that's exactly what I was coming to realize. From precancer to endometriosis, everything was making it more and more difficult to conceive and carry full term. Again, while I know this is what the doctors have to tell you, I felt like it was all too much to hear, too much to bear, and too much to deal with. I really just wanted my life back. I wanted to have a normal life of someone in her late 20s. Not having to worry about all of the effects of reproductive issues. Not having to live my life as planned by my menstrual cycle. Unfortunately, that was not the case for me. So I was left with this crossroad. Trying to decide if I wanted to continue treatment, or not.

One thing I failed to mention was Dr. M prescribed Lupron immediately following my operation by the other doctor. I was reluctant. I hate needles, I hate receiving injections, but all things pointed to Lupron as one of the leading "cures," per say, for endometriosis. It was fast acting and basically dissolved endometrial tumors. I felt like I really had no other choice other than to try this treatment. I was in so much pain, that all I could think of was that it's probably the best thing for me to go on this treatment even though I knew it could potentially make me sick, cause osteoporosis, or cause mood swings. So, I went for it.

In January of 2009, I went for my first round of treatment for Lupron. The impact was something far greater than I expected. All those warning signs and the warning labels and everything that you read about medication couldn't compare to the onslaught that it caused in my body. I was sick. I couldn't eat. I was depressed. Nothing seemed to help. I felt myself going in this downward spiral once again and I was so angry. Although the physical pain of the menstrual cycle was gone, the impact that the Lupron had on my mind and body was just as devastating.

I stopped the treatment after three months and things seemed to have gotten better. I finally had relief and felt like I was able to live a normal life. For about eight months, I had a fairly normal menstrual cycle. At least it was lighter. And I felt like God had finally blessed me with a cure, with some relief. The relief I felt like I deserved after dealing with this or these conditions for two decades.

Much to my dismay, in early 2010, many of these symptoms returned. The heavy periods came back, fatigue, excessive bleeding, irregular cycles, they were all back. At the time I was living in Atlanta, GA. I had just started my first full-time job in the sports information industry. I was excited. I was thrilled to be going after my dream career. I kept pushing forward, even though I noticed my body beginning to change again. The weight was back on, and I knew I had to do something to change this course. I changed my diet. I stopped eating out as much, I made sure that even on road trips I had a lunch box or something to carry snacks or even home cooked meals in. I was prepared to fight for my life. I saw several physicians in the Atlanta area.

After a year in Atlanta, I had moved to Kentucky and became the Sports Information Director at Kentucky State University. This, I thought, would be something new, something for me to start over. Maybe I just needed to change the environment that I was in, that would help my health? But, things got worse. I continued to experience heavy bleeding, I continued to experience severe pain and I remember at one point going back to the doctor for a check up, and fighting through the decision of whether or not to have surgery. At this point, I just couldn't. I didn't want to anymore. I didn't want to deal with another operations. I just had two major operations in one year and felt like my body needed a break. I remember speaking with my gynecologist there and she said, "What can we do? We need to do something. What are you willing to do?" I said, "you are the physician, tell me what I can do." And she looked at me and said, "it looks like Lupron is going to be your best bet." And she said, "you've had it once before, so you know what to expect," but did I? Once again, the injections started, and my body went into a complete frenzy. It was like chaos ensued. My digestive system, my urinary tract system, everything; my hormones, my mood, my appetite, everything was in complete disarray.

It all came to a head one night when one of my best friends was in town to visit me. We had just cooked this wonderful meal and we were sitting down watching TV, laughing and joking around. Within a couple of hours, I felt horrible. I was sick to my stomach and nauseous. My stomach was cramping so badly that I could hardly catch my breath. And I remember saying to her, "there's something not right," and I remember the fear in her eyes, the terror in her face, and the nervousness in her voice of trying to figure out what to do.

Finally, we made the call. I was headed to the ER. I remember being in the hospital bed and them giving me a shot of Zofran to help with nausea and stomach cramping. I was given some pain meds through an IV and given fluids. The pain subsided and I was taken back for the MRI. The MRI showed a partial blockage in one of my intestines. Apparently we had gotten to the hospital just in time because if things would have progressed, if I would've ignored the pain and just thought to drink more water, then I would've had a full blockage and they would have had to cut a portion of my intestine. And I thought, this is all due to the Lupron. I never had any of these issues with my digestive system before the Lupron, but, I couldn't have imagined that it would have gotten this bad. A blockage? In my intestine? From some medicine? The very thing that was supposed to make me better, the very thing that was supposed to help ease my pain, was actually causing more pain and more issues. All I could think was, "I don't want this anymore. I don't want another round of Lupron. I don't want another round of injections. I don't want to be tested and poked and prodded for anything else. I don't want another diagnosis or anything. I just want to be normal."

I finished that round of Lupron and I remember one time I went home and someone looked at me and said, "are you sick?" I gave them a little insight as to what was going on and it was at that moment I realized that the health issues I was having was causing more than a physical pain, it was actually causing physical changes in my body to the point where I looked like I was unhealthy. I did not look well. And that was one of the hardest things to deal with. Having people come up to you and ask "are you sick?", "what's wrong with you?" I think the people meant it out of the goodness of their hearts, but didn't know how to express the shock in what they saw, but it didn't help me. It didn't make me feel any better. It didn't make me feel good about myself. It didn't make feel like I was recovering. It actually had the opposite effect on me. I became more paranoid about how I looked, I became more concerned with my physical appearance. I tried to supplement how I looked and how I felt by wearing makeup, spending money on my hair and nails. I tried adjusting physical things to make myself feel better. But there was an internal pain that couldn't be fixed by making up my outward appearance. There was an internal pain that had to be healed internally. The problem was, I didn't know where to begin. I didn't know where to start. I had no idea what was next.

I think it was always in the back of my mind that I'd be dealing with this for the rest of my life. I wasn't really sure how I felt about it, to be honest. There were times where I was very happy that I knew exactly what was going on with my body and then there were times where I was extremely mad, sad, and uncertain about my future. I really didn't understand how your body could just turn against you like this. I remember having thoughts on what it would be like to have the life of a normal 20-something-year-old. My life was far from normal. It was always, always, in the back of my mind that I'd always have to be prepared for the unexpected with my body.

The Lupron continued to do a number on me. It caused incontinence and mood swings. I remember going to the gynecologist one day and telling her, "there's something wrong. I can't hold my bladder. I can't hold my bowels. I'm sad all the time. I never felt like this before I started taking the Lupron." Her response to me was short, lacking compassion, and pretty 'matter of fact'. She said, "Lupron doesn't cause those things." and that was it. To me, she didn't believe me. There was nothing I said from that point on to make her believe that I was experiencing the symptoms I was because of the Lupron. At one point she told me that it sounded like I was reading the warning signs off of the medication label or from WebMD and reciting it back to her. I was shocked, and obviously upset. The last thing I needed was another doctor that didnt believe what I was telling them about what was going on with my own body. I knew my body. I knew how it responded to things. This was not it, at all. I was sick. I needed help. I needed a doctor that believed what I was telling them was going on, not someone that passed it off as me reading the label or the warning signs or side effects of some medication and saying this is what I have. I was not a hypochondriac by any stretch of the imagination. I just needed a doctor that believed me. She was not the one. So again, rather than going back to her, I continued to suffer until I couldn't anymore. And then, another red flag. The same symptoms I was experiencing in late 2008 when I had the surgery for precancer, those exact symptoms resurfaced.

In 2011, I tested positive again for abnormal cells. This time, on my cervix and a little lesion on the outside of my vulva. They were able to simply remove the abnormal cells without surgery, thank God. The last thing I wanted was another operation for the same stuff, but, I figured that at least they caught it early where they were able to simply remove the cells through a biopsy rather than having to operate. They kept a close watch on it. Being in Kentucky and away from family, I was nervous about needing operation after operation. So I chose to steer clear of operations. The heavy periods returned. This time, even worse. I was passing large clots every single month. Sometimes the clots were half the size of my palm and other times about the size of my thumb. Sometimes they were just little dots. But, the heavier the periods became, the more I felt like I was doomed and this was just something I was going to have to live through and with for the rest of my life. I really saw no end, especially having a doctor that didn't believe I was experiencing the things I was.

Let's fast forward a little bit. I went to Cincinnati in 2012, I started working at the University of Cincinnati and started seeing one of their specialists at the UC Hospital. At that point, I gave them the full rundown of my medical history, they had all my files.

I was intent on finding more natural ways to handle what I was dealing with. I made it through 2012, or so I thought.

I made it to the end of the year with nothing. I was ecstatic about that. Around April of 2013 the severely heavy bleeding, and large blood clots returned. I now had a great gynecologist. She was very attentive to my needs and I told her about my history. Obviously, she had my files, but, I was still intent upon explaining things from my perspective. She assured me that they would do everything they could to take care of my needs. They've seen severe cases of endometriosis before, they were going to take care of me. They put me back on birth control, which I felt like, this time around, was working a little better, but then I started bleeding uncontrollably again, nonstop for a month. I went to the doctor and said, this is what happened to me in 2008. And she said, "this normally does not happen it could be the hormones or your body adjusting to the hormones. You do have a severe hormonal imbalance but let's take you off birth control." I thought, "Great." I stopped taking birth control but in April of 2013, my symptoms returned and again, I was bleeding through my clothes. I was uncomfortable, fatigued, and looking for relief. The suggestion? Lupron.

To be honest, at this point I had done my research. I knew that there really wasn't much else they can do beyond Lupron and birth control. It was the patch, it was the pill, some sort of birth control. I agreed, reluctantly, but I still agreed.

My body, my hormones and my emotions went through another swing of things. And I remember thinking to myself that the last thing I want is another blockage in my intestine. So I went to a raw diet for a week before treatment started. I ate nothing but fruits and vegetables and then when the treatment started, with weeks of doing research, I found that I could make my own juice, so I started juicing. I pretty much lived off apple, carrot, ginger juice. It was great for having an upset stomach or having digestive issues. I found that to be a great help for the nausea and upset stomach that I was getting from the Lupron.

I felt crazy going back to the doctor and telling her that I'm having these issues again- like my bladder was uncontrollable. At one point I started wearing Depends because I could not afford to be in the middle of my work day or at a sporting event and have a leak or worse. And so I made the decision to once again to change up my wardrobe to hide the fact I was wearing adult diapers. Even though they say you can't see them, they're there, and you know they're there. They're uncomfortable and so I made sure that no one could tell. I wore clothes that would hide the ruffling sound the Depends made, but my life was still not normal. I was still experiencing things that at my age I never imagined that I would be going through. And I was angry.

I was mad about dealing with the same problem five years later, I was still dealing with the same thing. Still dealing with the same issues. I had another precancer scare in the summer but the doctor was able to do a simple procedure and I was in the clear.

In November of 2013, I had left the University of Cincinnati and I was back at Kentucky State University. I noticed that my my body again was changing. I had a new gynecologist, I explained my history, she had my medical records. I was ready for something more permanent, something that was really going to help me get over this hump. But the bleeding would not stop. The only thing that was helping, the only thing that kept me from passing large clots, from bleeding heavily, from bleeding through my clothes, from being fatigued to the point where I couldn't function was the Lupron. So in September 2013, I started Lupron again, but this time it was to get over the hump.

I let the doctor know that I really did not want to do it, but I also could not stand to bleed uncontrollably or to have such an unpredictable cycle. Something had to change though, I had this new job, I had a great new career path, I had a loving church family, and I met one of my very best friends at the church and he and I were working together on so many different things. Work was phenomenal and I had come back to Kentucky and now I was back in the same area with my best friend. I had all these great things happening around me, but inside I was suffering. I was depressed, I was sick, and I just didn't feel like myself. We'll get to that in the next chapter. Right now, I want to continue focusing on the physical side of things.

By November 2013, I was in Chicago with my family for Thanksgiving and probably two weeks or so before that I had some of the same symptoms precancer recurring. I went to the doctor, they did a biopsy, and it was the waiting game. This call came through the day after Thanksgiving and the voicemail stated that precancer cells were back and I need treatment. I remember being there with my family and being devastated and scared because all I could think was, "again? why? why now?" I've done everything I could to keep all this stuff from happening, I've changed my diet. I've been exercising more. I've been taking my supplements and treating my body right. I was getting my flu and pneumonia shots and getting all of these vaccines. I took all of the preventive precautions, but it wouldn't stop. It kept coming back.

When I returned to Kentucky, I had to start on a topical treatment to get rid of the cells. This treatment was horrible! It makes your skin flake and fall off. The skin continues to fall off until the treatment is done. It burns. It was just awful, especially for someone who's skin in certain areas was open and cracked, so putting this treatment on top of what was already open just exacerbated what I was feeling. Physically, it was uncomfortable, it was painful. I again was spending time showing up to work late because I couldn't sleep at night and I would finally fall asleep and it would be time to get up. Or I was having to go back in the middle of the day to wash up and get myself cleaned up because of the fact that this treatment was causing other reactions in my body. And it was something that is not on the warning labels, you're not going to see that it could cause a fever, or more, but at one point I had a fever and felt like it was due to the medication that I was on and my body constantly trying to fight off all of these things that were being put into it that were foreign objects.

My body was trying to fight off the things that didn't belong in it as well as fight itself. There were several times I was sick and had flu-like symptoms but had no flu virus. I never had a positive flu test, but I had fevers and headaches and body aches and all this other stuff. All I could think was "it's this medication." The constant manipulation of natural processes in my body was causing additional issues, but I felt like there was nothing I could do. I felt I had to deal with flu-like symptoms in order to get a grasp on everything else.

The doctors were telling me otherwise. And I had put so much trust in the doctors, so much trust in what they were telling me to do, I looked at them as the experts and when they didn't believe me, I internalized that and allowed that to be something that kept me from really verbalizing what I was dealing with. I think subconsciously, it was because I didn't want another doctor to reject me, or to tell me I was making up this stuff. I could pinpoint literally every symptom I was having to when a treatment started, to when a test performed, a pelvic exam, a biopsy, or something.

When I returned from Thanksgiving break, they had to do another biopsy. They were able to remove the cells from the cervix, again, they tested those, and those came back negative. They were slightly abnormal, but nothing was alarming. So I continued with the treatment until it was over, and felt like I was in the clear. In December of 2013, I lost my job and moved to Chicago to live with my brother and his family. I was there for about seven months. I saw a gynecologist and an endocrinologist to help me with everything. At that point was so tired physically and emotionally, that I wanted everything to be done. I was not pressed about starting Lupron again. I didn't care to start it again. I was, in my mind, completely over it and done.

As fate would have it, I moved back to Ohio in July of 2014 and I was working at a private school in Akron. Then my reproductive issues resurfaced *again*. The heavy bleeding, blood clots, the fatigue, and they were worse this time. I knew the doctor was probably going to suggest Lupron, but again, I was not prepared for that and really didn't want to have to deal with it. So, since I was back in the Cleveland area, I went back to seeing Dr. M., as she was the specialist who helped most. I trusted her. When I was telling her things that were going on in my body, she listened. That is the type of doctor we all need.

I remember waking up and having this awful breast pain. It felt like my right breast was absolutely on fire. I felt it in my arm, I felt it in my armpit, I felt it down the side of my body. At this point, I had already been diagnosed with fibrocystic breast disease (FBD). I felt like the FBD was a diagnosis that the doctor in Kentucky gave me because they had no idea what else was going on. The mammogram performed when I was in Kentucky was a means of giving me some sort of diagnosis. But there's really nothing they can do when you have FBD, they just tell you to stay away from caffeine. And if you want, you can take some of the medication they would give someone who has fibromyalgia. Again, not much help. I was not willing to take any other medications because I had been on so many other treatments before. I didn't want to keep putting my body into shock.

They performed a breast exam and confirmed that the lump I thought I was feeling, was actually there, and I faced another operation. In October 2014, I had a lumpectomy on my right breast. I waited two weeks and the test results came back that the lump was benign. I was ecstatic. I remember celebrating with my family, sending a picture to my brother and sister-in-law, my parents, my best friends, cheering and ecstatic that this time, it's benign! It wasn't even precancerous. There were no traces of abnormalities. It was a benign tumor.

My breasts, since then, have been in the clear, thank God. Unfortunately, I have this really ugly scar on it. It reminds me of yet another battle that I've been through. The good thing is, like all of the others, I overcame it. I conquered it. I thought that was going to be the start of some healing. But, I soon realized that things were getting worse.

In 2015, I made a job change and started working at the school I'm at now as well as as a temp at a well-known nonprofit organization. Though my health issues continued to overwhelm me in various instances, I knew that I couldn't give up. I wanted to give up on several occasions, I wanted to throw in the towel. It was really difficult to explain to people that the physical pain I was feeling was not made up. It was real and something I had to push through every moment of the day. It was exasperated because I couldn't sleep enough. This was something deeper. This was my body turning against me. This was me fighting off stuff that I felt I shouldn't have to fight off.

In 2015, after I switched jobs, I was working at the school, living on campus, and I remember one night I was bleeding so heavily, I had to go back to the ER. I passed a huge clot and the bleeding afterwards was intense and unrelenting. All I could think was "get to the hospital." I got to the hospital and of course they said it's just your menstrual cycle, so there's really nothing we can do. Nothing you can do? How is that possible? Can't you give me something that would stop the bleeding? No. There was nothing I could do. I was told to follow up with my gynecologist and maybe they would put me back on Lupron, maybe they would give me birth control again. But according to them, there was really nothing they could provide that would assist with the pain or bleeding.

After a few hours in the ER, I was sent home and told to rest, take pain medicine, and I was given a prescription for a muscle relaxer. The muscle relaxant was supposed to help with the cramping, and

I took it every night for about two weeks. But it left me groggy and feeling worse than I did by not sleeping. I was completely lethargic and honestly felt pretty useless at work. I was struggling just to make it through the day, but what other options did I have?

It was 2015 and, at this point, I had been dealing with this since I was nine years old. That's right- 24 years. 24 years of reproductive issues. What's next? What's next for someone who after 24 years still has no relief? I kept pushing, but it got worse.

In January 2016, I was back at the hospital. I had once again taken myself to the ER because I was bleeding so heavily, and passing such large clots, that I knew something was wrong. Of course they always tried to tell you that I was probably pregnant or having a miscarriage. And dealing with doctors constantly thinking I'm pregnant and lying about it caused other emotional issues that you don't realize until you get past it and think to yourself, "this really had a negative impact on me."

In April 2016, I began to see another doctor because, by this point, the first specialist I was seeing had become so busy, between her teaching, and her patient load, it was sometimes two or three months before I could get in to her. My first visit with Dr. K was April 28, 2016. She was gentle. She was kind. She was compassionate. She also let me know that we needed to try the Lupron again because she was concerned for my overall well-being and quality of life. So, the beginning of May, I started my last round of Lupron, and she made it very clear that this would be my last round because she was concerned that my bones had begun to show loss of density.

We agreed that if I did not improve at the end of the treatment, if there was still pain at the end of or throughout the treatment, that she would stop the injections and operate to clear out endometriosis and endometrial tumors and cysts that were present. Another operation. How many operations can one body take? I thought in my feeble, maybe even naive, mind that this many operations were for people who had severe health issues like cancer or needed a transplant or had other severe, debilitating illnesses that would cause them to need an amputation or heart surgery. I had none of that. I was so confused by the fact that year after year I was dealing with the same exact issues and going through the same treatments without relief. Nevertheless, in July 2016, I went through another operation. They cleared out endometriosis and removed endometrial tumors and cysts that were present. Once again, I was on the road to recovery.

I continued to see Dr. K. One thing I failed to mention previously was that as these issues progressed and endometriosis spread, I was experiencing muscle spasms in my abdomen as well as anal spasms (which they call the levator system). So, I was faced with another decision, they wanted to treat the muscle spasms because they continued to worsen. There were several times where I would be out and about and the muscle spasms would completely overcome me. One time I was in Atlanta, visiting friends, and preparing for ministry. I remember it was the night before we were set to preach and I had a severe attack. My legs and lower back were like rocks. I had to be helped in and out of the car and I thought at one point that I wasn't going to be able to preach.

All I could do the night before was rest and pray. All I needed was for God to help me make it through. Somehow, He did it. The end result was me flying home and making another appointment with Dr. K, explaining to her the symptoms that I was feeling. Unfortunately, she wanted to operate again. They were also interested in testing me for deep endometriosis where endometrial tumors or nodules actually grow on your rectum causing severe spasms and other issues with bowel movements and incontinence.

I was not excited, and I even tried to put it off. but in February 2017, it was back to the operating room. I had no choice. There were certain things I was willing to do because I wanted the relief. I got some relief for a while. But then the symptoms returned and I felt like I was unable to function.

In March 2017, I was seen by Dr. M. and one of her colleagues Dr. B., regarding my issues. I was also seen by Dr. K. I needed someone to tell me something so that I could start to feel better. I was ready for a change. I was ready for a pain free life that I had never experienced before. I didn't know what it was like to live pain free. I knew it existed and I was ready to go after it. I believed that I deserved a life of what I perceived to be that of a normal 30-something woman. I was 35 years old. I had my whole life ahead of me. I had so many things I wanted to do and accomplish. I wanted to see the world. I wanted to travel. I felt like my reproductive issues were holding me back from really experiencing life to the fullest.

March 2017, I had another procedure where they were able to do another pelvic exam, an ultrasound, an MRI, and a mammogram. All to make sure that nothing had progressed beyond endometriosis. So time went on, Dr. K refused to put me on Lupron again; I was grateful for that, but, I was also a little concerned because I really didn't know what to expect. All I had was birth control. She decided to take me off of birth control and put me on a medication that would help ease the pain. She sent me to a pelvic pain specialist through the Cleveland Clinic for pelvic pain physical therapy, but it wasn't enough. They told me I needed to try it even more, but as I went through the pelvic pain therapy, and I did the kegels and pelvic exercises, the pain increased and the clots passed more frequently. I had dropped almost 30 pounds since the very first operation in 2010. I was doing everything I could. I even went to a vegan diet for six months followed by a vegetarian diet for nearly one year. I was taking my health into my own hands, but it just didn't seem like it was enough… then it happened again.

In August 2017, I went in for an office visit because I had the signs and symptoms of precancer. I knew the signs; I knew the itching, the burning. I knew the feeling that it gave. By this time I was able to tell the difference between a yeast infection and the symptoms of precancerous cells returning. I was diligent. I frequently examined myself to make sure everything was ok. It was the only reassurance that I could give myself that, at the very least, I was very conscientious about my health. Everything seemed to be failing, so self-examinations were what I felt I had control over. Some days, I checked myself 10 times because I was paranoid that I would miss something major. The physical issues were really impacting my mental stability.

August 22, 2017 I went to see the oncologist again. He confirmed one of my worst fears. Precancerous cells had in fact come back and this time they were at a stage where they could not be ignored. I either needed surgery or I needed to try the topical treatment again. So I tried the topical treatment again. I was miserable. It was the worst feeling that I had when it came to treatments, next to the Lupron. This topical treatment burned. There were several times where I'd try to take it at night and then take a melatonin so that I could let the medicine work and sleep through it. But it wasn't working. I was waking up in the middle of the night and I had blood in my fingernails and on my hands because I was scratching myself in my sleep, which caused more open wounds and more thickened skin. When I went back to see him, we decided on surgery. So on December 18, 2017, I had surgery again for precancer cells.

Let's keep in mind that while dealing with precancer, I was still battling the severe issues related to endometriosis and I want to back up for a second, because before the last operation in February 2017, I received an additional diagnosis that's related to endometriosis. They diagnosed me with adenomyosis. Adenomyosis is very similar to endometriosis but this illness is when the inner lining of the uterus actually breaks through the muscular wall of the uterus and grows and becomes intertwined within the uterine wall. Adenomyosis also causes severe cramps, bloating, heavy periods, and it can also cause heavy and abnormal bleeding, as well as severe pain. Now I was dealing with adenomyosis and endometriosis. Keeping in mind that endometriosis was growing down and attaching to nerves in an area that was very close to my rectum, which was causing a lot of the anal spasms I experienced. But I was also getting spasms in my hips and abdomen and my legs as a result of endometriosis and then the adenomyosis diagnosis came. It's treatable, but, the only way you can get rid of it it is through a hysterectomy.

Well, I was unmarried and without kids. The last thing I wanted was a hysterectomy. But in February 2017, the necessity of a hysterectomy became palpable for me. It was the first time that that word had really been put out there as an option for treatment. And I put it off. I knew that I had these endometrial tumors growing, I knew I had cysts that kept developing, I knew that I was having blood clots that were getting larger and more difficult to pass because of adenomyosis and endometriosis, but I fought. I came off of all medication. I stopped taking certain treatments and decided that I was going to let my body do what it could to heal itself. I lost weight and I continued to exercise and try to take care of my body the best I could, but even that became difficult because moving hurt. I was extremely fatigued.

I had gotten off of work one evening and finally gotten in bed and was laying there and all of a sudden, this incredible pain hit me. I stood up to go to the bathroom and all of a sudden a blood clot the size of my palm passes and I started bleeding out of control again. I was prepared to take myself to the hospital. I was in excruciating pain, the bleeding would not stop, the cramping would not stop. A couple of my coworkers saw me and immediately said "No. you're not driving yourself anywhere." As embarrassed as I was, I knew that I needed help. I allowed my coworker to take me to the hospital, and he stayed with me the entire night. I finally got back to a room and again they told me "there's nothing that we can do for you. This will continue unless you have a hysterectomy." I'm not having a hysterectomy! There's no way! I'll just have to bleed, I'll just deal with this pain. A hysterectomy? They can't be serious. This was just two months after my 36th birthday. The last thing I was going to deal with was not being able to have kids at all. And of course people were telling me be faithful and keep the faith and keep pressing. "This isn't what God wants for you," some people said. Well, I didn't believe that God wants me to live in pain either, but I couldn't wrap my head around having a hysterectomy when I didn't have kids and had never been married. It was crazy to me. I nixed the idea immediately.

After surgery in December, it was back to the drawing board for me. The pain continued. I felt horrible. The last visit to the emergency room came in April 2018, when my coworker took me. A month later, I was scheduled for my hysterectomy. Getting to that point was one of the most painful decisions I've had to make. But it was either that or know that this adenomyosis was going to continue causing so much pain and even though adenomyosis itself is not life threatening, some of the pain that it causes and the impact that it has, could be life threatening. There were times where I would be driving and would be doubled over in my car and it would take everything in me to slow my car down and pull off to the side of the road. These are the things people *don't* tell you. These are the things *we're not talking enough about.* These are the things that *people are not telling women about their reproductive health.*

I was fatigued, I was dizzy a lot of times, I was nauseous, I had a loss of appetite. Yet, they never talk about how reproductive issues are linked to mental health issues. But I'm here to talk about it. I'm here to open pandora's box on this discussion that health (physical, mental, emotional, spiritual) issues are intertwined. I was not diabetic until the issues with the severe bleeding in 2008. I was a healthy person. I was working out. Yes, I was overweight at the time, but nothing in my history pointed to diabetes other than my heredity. But we don't talk about it enough, so women tend to suffer in silence and in humiliation because we're too afraid to talk about these issues. The fact of the matter is, if we advocate for ourselves, we can help other women advocate for themselves. We can talk about the fact that I know beyond a shadow of doubt what Lupron did to my body. I know what birth control did to my body. I know what these treatments did to my body. Despite not being believed by two doctors, I was still able to make the best decision for me. And it is not a decision I am comfortable with even as I write this book. I still have emotional and spiritual pain from making that decision. But we have to get to the point where we begin to believe women.

There's no amount of money that can cause a doctor to believe you. They didn't believe Gabrielle Union, they didn't believe Serena Williams, they didn't believe Kim Porter. These women are (were) millionaires and doctors did not believe them. My hope is that, in sharing my story, women become relentless in advocating for themselves. Don't stop going to the doctor just because one does not believe you. I know firsthand that, even though we must be relentless in our self-advocacy, nothing removes the emotional, spiritual, and mental pain inflicted by battling severe reproductive issues.

❖ Mental Pain

I mentioned before when talking about the physical pain that comes with endometriosis, adenomyosis, and precancer how those issues ultimately led to me needing a hysterectomy. I did not need a hysterectomy because my life was in imminent danger, but my quality of life had deteriorated so much over the years that it was impacting every facet of my life - from activity planning and work-life balance to even just being able to work.

One thing I wish there was more discussion about is how endometriosis and reproductive issues are linked to a woman's mental health. It could be anything from managing the pain to not being believed by doctors. Sometimes, it just takes one person to fully believe in you and what you're going through. What I experienced was a deep loneliness. I was surrounded by loved ones and people who supported me, helped me, prayed for me, but in this battle, I felt alone.

In 2013 there was a perfect storm for me. I was fired from one job and went right into working another job. I should have been happy, pleased and filled with joy. I really had a great life set-up - good healthcare, great home church, involved on campus and in the community, one of my best friends lived in the area. I was in an environment and place in my life where everything looked perfect and happy. But I was miserable.

In October 2013 I was diagnosed with depression, anxiety and OCD. Prior to that, I never thought anything was wrong with me. I just took my emotions as being an overly emotional person. As I went through some of these issues at the end of 2017 and through 2018, I realized what I was experiencing with my reproductive health had deeply affected my mental health and spiritual health (which we get into later).

Depression is defined as feeling sad for a few days, lacking motivation for daily activities, losing interest in daily activities and things that usually excite you, and even mild mood swings. It also may involve anxiety. I cannot express how profoundly chronic health issues infringe upon our mental health. Reproductive illness caused (what seemed to be) insurmountable stress—to the point where I felt like nothing I was doing was going to be good enough. The distress made me believe I was diseased and incurable.

In a way, I was. There is no cure for endometriosis, adenomyosis or precancerous processes. And for endometriosis and adenomyosis, there is no known cause. While there are things that point to increased risk for these two conditions, there is nothing finite to say one thing or another causes these debilitating diseases. When you have a condition or disease where there is no end in sight because there is no cure, it weighs on you, heavily. Sometimes you don't realize how heavy or it clicks and it has gone on for so long you don't recognize yourself.

When you're going through chronic illness, there is no light at the end of the tunnel. You cannot see the "end" because there is no cure and you don't know if the next round of treatment is going to do the trick for you. The anguish piles up when you go to the doctor and are told the only other option is a hysterectomy because, medically, they've done everything they could for you and you could risk having endometrial cysts rupture. Your refusal to take hard painkillers (Vicodin, OxyContin, etc.) could mean other injuries due to pain (collapsing, fainting due to loss of blood, or worse). I had to make the hard choice to either live through the pain, or live the high life of taking narcotics to regulate the pain. *But I wanted to LIVE UNINHIBITED!* I had no desire to be in pain but also did not want to be a zombie. So, I chose the pain.

To a greater degree, a hysterectomy was the only way to get rid of adenomyosis, which was the main cause of the pain, the large clots and heavy bleeding. They cannot operate and cut out adenomyosis because it damages the uterus. The only way to remove adenomyosis is to remove your entire uterus. In that instance, in hearing that news, I went from believing and having hope that, if I held out a little longer, tried the next best treatment, popped this other pill, ate this vegetable, drank this concoction, or lost this amount of weight—if I just had faith—I would overcome everything from despair to feeling utterly defeated.

There's this endless battle within you to keep trying—an endless battle within you to never give up and to keep pushing because there could be something out there that cures you. There could be something out there to help you get over the hump and at least overcome one of your health issues. Let's not forget that through all this I am diabetic. My blood sugar was out of control sometimes. My numbers would shoot through the roof and then crash. It was not an issue with my diet. I kept telling my doctor I believe endometriosis is directly connected to me being diabetic.

I spent a great deal of time reading articles about endometriosis, diabetes and chronic illnesses. I had a firm grasp on the fact that women with endometriosis were more susceptible to other chronic illnesses, including diabetes. Unfortunately, there was no firm, clinical connection between endo and diabetes. Nearly every doctor told me there was no connection and I needed to manage my weight for diabetes and manage the pain for endo. One doctor told me I was in fact at a higher risk for diabetes but endometriosis did not cause it. Another doctor told me it was possible that endometriosis led to me being diabetic. It was overwhelming at times trying to convince medical professionals what I believed. But it seemed they just wanted to tell me to lose weight and manage the pain. Didn't they understand how hard weight management was with endo?

My conditions were directly tied to the metabolic and endocrine systems. While the connection between the two made sense to me - I was not diabetic until the severe endo was discovered - it was like another slap in the face to fight doctors who did not believe me enough to dig deeper in their own research and practice to help me. Ever since then, I've had issues controlling my weight and blood sugar.

The combination of trying to balance diabetes and reproductive illnesses led me into a space of feeling even more alone and hopeless. It was like there was no end. I even felt that I was being punished. I just couldn't wrap my head around it all. It was all a huge burden on me. Even worse, I felt like I was a burden for others. The sadness, excruciating pain, discomfort and increasing fatigue made daily activities feel like hard labor and because of that, there were times I felt like I needed help from others to do things like clean the house. I was too embarrassed to even consider asking for help with simple tasks. I determined in my head that needing help was burdensome for others, even though I had not reached out to anyone. People were not always understanding either.

As I got to the point where a hysterectomy was my only option, I began to grieve the loss of fertility. I grieved deeply. I felt like a failure. I wanted nothing more than to have kids. I dreamt of having a starting lineup for a basketball team—that's how many kids I wanted—and all boys! There were times I thought about just getting pregnant, at least trying, so my dream wouldn't escape me.

But then I thought being unmarried and pregnant would bring shame to my family. It would be an embarrassment for my family for me to be pregnant, yet unmarried. I also thought, depending on how I chose to conceive, people would question my character and whether or not I was in sin or knew who the father of my child was. All these emotions, feelings and thoughts I had influenced my emotional and mental health.

The issues I was dealing with then and dealt with all the way through December 2018 were HARD and caused a great deal of grief. There were times where I was depressed and couldn't figure out what was going on. I would be so sad, crying for days and not knowing or understanding why. Things would snowball and I would become even more upset because I couldn't pinpoint the source of my sadness. I had no idea it was a buildup from years of battling illnesses.

I couldn't get and stay happy. One minute I would be happy and the next something would not go right and I would feel like a failure. I couldn't overcome the feeling of loneliness and that, after every operation, there was a timeframe where I lost my independence and couldn't do simple stuff like tie my own shoes. I couldn't shower without having someone there to monitor me in case there were complications.

The first two months after my hysterectomy were scary. During the operation, I had subconjunctival hemorrhaging in both eyes, causing me to have blurred vision for days and loss of peripheral vision for about a month. My eyes were so red, I looked like I had been on a bender for days. My blood pressure shot up during surgery, causing my eyes to hemorrhage (at least that is the explanation I was given, but they were not completely sure).

After the operation I had in December 2017, I had a fall. I had gotten up to use the bathroom one morning and as I was getting off the toilet, I became disoriented and dizzy and fell. I was lying on the cold floor in the bathroom, crying and trying to scream for help. At one point, I could hear my dad's footsteps in the kitchen, so I took the toilet paper holder and used it to bang on the floor. When I heard him go back into their bedroom, I broke down in tears. I kept screaming for help and banging the toilet paper holder on the floor. I heard his footsteps in the kitchen again, so I banged the metal to the floor a little harder and faster and wailed a little louder.

I stopped the banging when I heard him upstairs and relinquished my efforts to tears. I was lying on the cold floor, half naked with a wet face. My dad yelled for my mom to come help. They covered me with a blanket and rolled me over so my mom could pull up my pants, then helped me to my feet. They got me back in bed and I rested. As I was lying in bed, I was saddened by the situation — not being able to help myself, not having the strength to get up, and wondering if I at least had the strength to crawl to the bedroom where someone could better hear my cry for help.

It is moments like what I just described that we need to talk about. It's moments like that, when you're feeling helpless and when, even as someone who is very independent and typically the one who takes care of others, you feel unable to take care of yourself. We need to openly discuss exactly how our emotional and mental health can be degraded by physical health issues. I was miserable. It was a daily struggle to look at myself through the eyes of those who loved and cared for me. I did not feel I was worthy of that love and care, not because I had done anything to them, but because my conditions seemed to be such a strain. I felt I deserved to be alone so that I wouldn't cause others any distress. Much of what I was feeling became exasperated by the physical pain, sleep deprivation and not really having anyone who understood what was going on.

I decided to seek counseling, despite everything stigma tells us about mental health. If you listen to what society tells you, people will make you think you're crazy and imagining things. The church, well they'll tell you to pray and have faith. But what society and the church miss the mark on many times is telling you it's okay not to be okay and it is also okay to get help.

I had gotten to the point where I sought out counseling from various sources. I was desperate for something to help me sort through my feelings and thoughts while I worked with doctors to manage the illnesses. I wanted peace and to get to a place where I could deal with the decisions I had to make — even prior to the hysterectomy.

Endometriosis and other issues caused me to feel very insecure. I often felt ugly and unattractive because my weight had become uncontrollable and I had hit a plateau where I was no longer losing weight. In December 2018, the day I found out I needed surgery to remove precancerous cells again, I found out my weight had ballooned up to 151 pounds. That was the heaviest I had been in the last ten years, and it had all happened in about one month.

I felt like I couldn't face myself. I would look in the mirror and not recognize who I was, because I didn't want to see the person who was dealing with all this stuff. I didn't look healthy, I didn't feel healthy. I was angry, and I was hurt. I felt like life had gotten the best of me and there was too much for me to overcome. I remember in the month before my December 2018 operation, I called my dad, because I knew he understood what it was like to fight a battle where sometimes you don't see the end.

In December 2018, I allowed myself to let go and freely feel every emotion and to call on others to discuss what I was going through, rather than repress everything in the name of being strong. I realized it takes more strength to admit what's going on, to seek help, and be consistent with getting help, than it does to repress and pretend everything is okay. I understood my physical ailments had overcome me, but the mental side was something we just don't talk about enough. We internalize these issues and think, "This is me. This is something I will just have to deal with on my own." Meanwhile, we cannot go out in public without having paranoia set in about bleeding through our clothes, wondering if we have a bad odor. As you may know, when you bleed a lot, the smell of blood can be putrid. I kept more hygiene items in my purse than anything else and at the slightest smell, I was running to the nearest bathroom to freshen up. During my workday, I would sometimes go back to my apartment or to a faculty locker room to shower.

I was completely paranoid and sometimes would imagine that things were happening that were not. For instance, many times I would have the sensation of blood or urine dripping down my legs or waking up in the middle of the night because I wanted to make sure I had not bled through anything. It weighs on you. It impacts your mental health at a level that must be discussed. There is absolutely nothing wrong with you. These are natural feelings. God has wired us to be emotional beings and dealing with depression, paranoia, and needing therapy and support from others is okay!

Don't ever think there is something wrong with you because you need to see a therapist or join a support group to deal with the thoughts and feelings related to your infertility or chronic ill-ness(es). You are human. My hope and prayer is that when we are dealing with the thoughts and feelings related to endometriosis, adenomyosis, polycystic ovarian syndrome (PCOS), and infertility, we remember it's okay not to be okay and it's okay to seek therapy.

There are a wide variety of techniques that help with grief, infertility, and reproductive-related depression (eg. postpartum depression). I found a great sense of comfort in reading blogs, articles and the discussions in web-based forums and groups. I liked the privacy and was comforted by the fact that there were women experiencing the exact same thing as me and agreeing that what works for one of us may not work for others.

Reading scholarly articles about reproductive health also helped me make decisions that were best and process some of the things I was feeling and thinking. Not everyone feels helped in the same way, so it's critical to find what works best for you and remain consistent in applying those mechanisms.

Endometriosis affects about 10 percent of women of reproductive age and is one of the leading causes of chronic pelvic pain in women. One of the articles I read in the May 2017 issue of the *International Journal of Women's Health* talks about anxiety and depression in patients with endometriosis and the challenges associated with managing endo. One thing that stuck out to me was the fact that high levels of anxiety and depression can amplify the severity of pain. It went on to say that further studies are needed to understand the relationship between psychological factors and the perception of pain. But it doesn't say they're not related.

I remember two of my doctors didn't believe I was having any sort of psychological response to the treatments, pain or medication. It was made up in my head. The article dove a little deeper and showed that several studies link endo with psychological diseases.

I am not saying that just because you have endo or infertility issues that you have some sort of psychological disease or challenge, but it's important to understand one can impact the other. Your chronic illness can have psychological ramifications, cause stress, make you feel anxious and even depressed.

I felt this at a deeper level because it was a dream of mine to birth my own children. I wanted to physically conceive, carry and deliver a child, and dealing with that no longer being a possibility really caused emotions and feelings I was not prepared for. I questioned womanhood and felt like less of a woman. I struggled with the pros and cons of having a hysterectomy.

There was an internal battle of me saying, "You know you don't want this, but if you don't have a hysterectomy, something could happen that would be even worse than what you're experiencing now." I would then immediately think about getting pregnant but because of my reproductive issues I would not be able to carry the child to full term. Or what if some of the issues caused birth defects. How would I feel then? Would I be selfish because my desire to conceive, carry and deliver a child from my own body outweighed the potential dangers and health issues my child may face? As I weighed my options, one of the most significant deciding factors was the realization that I would never want to cause harm or endanger my child's health because of my own desires.

I didn't want to be a woman who was so bent on having her own child that she would put her child at risk. Even though there was nothing saying that would happen, I knew from the beginning it would always be a high-risk pregnancy. I knew there would be difficulties in conceiving and some of the other issues I had could have caused doctors to have to terminate my pregnancy if things progressed. That was something I could not deal with and refused to have weigh on me. I could not handle the thought of something going wrong because I went against doctors' warnings.

What's more is that nontraditional means of conceiving like IVF meant taking hormones and doing things that would have caused endometriosis to worsen. Hormones are to endometriosis what gasoline is to a fire: a raging, fury-filled scene that spreads if not treated properly.

I know there are other ways to have a child, to be a mother, but I wanted what I wanted. I had to learn to grieve the loss of not getting what I wanted and how I wanted it to happen. I experienced deep anxiety with having to make the decision to have a hysterectomy. It took me being hospitalized in April 2018 to get to the point where I said this is enough and this is not how I want to live. But it was not easy.

One night I fell at my parents house. I was walking into the kitchen after eating dinner and I fell to my knees and then fully on the ground writhing in pain. The pain was so severe and I could feel the clot passing. Pain would ruminate from my abdomen through the tips of my toes.

About a month before that, I was in church praising God and the praise turned into something else where I felt pain through my lower body. I was sick, faint, and weak. My pulse was low and my blood pressure had dropped significantly. I remember my dad kneeling down beside me once they got me into a wheelchair, and he said, "Are you just in pain?" I told him everything hurt, then I looked at him and said, "I am tired."

I remember him sobbing. We got to the nurses' area of the church and while they were monitoring my vitals, I felt the most intense sense of hopelessness. I felt like my entire body was turning against me and there was nothing I could do. At that moment, I wanted to throw in the towel. I felt defeated and there was nothing anyone could say or do to make me feel better.

It was like I was in a horrible nightmare. The pain and bleeding and fatigue made me feel depressed and the depression amplified the pain. I struggled to find resolve between what I was thinking and feeling and what was going on with my body physically. I wondered if there was an end to the vicious cycle of the pain causing depression and the depression causing pain.

There had to be a clear end to all of this, but what was it? What could possibly end everything without ending my life? I was not suicidal, but I was willing to do anything to get rid of the pain. I toyed with the idea of finding a way to purchase medicinal marijuana, but then I realized I couldn't take it because I work at a school and have a career that, no matter where I went, I would be drug tested. I didn't want to risk testing positive for anything.

I made a decision to learn coping mechanisms and ways to overcome the guilt of having a hysterectomy. The pain I was experiencing internally resulted in mental and emotional pain. I believed that if I learned how to manage my emotions, I could help myself deal with depression and learn warning signs of being in a depressed episode.

One sign for me was clutter. When my living space became cluttered, I knew I was in an episode. Once I noticed this, I would spend time cleaning and organizing to help bring me back to a sterile environment where I could focus. That was something I learned for myself, but as we deal with mental health, we need to understand our own red flags and be able to make a phone call and tell someone what we are feeling or thinking. I finally got to the point in 2018 where I was making calls to ask for help, ask to hang out, and expressing my feelings to my friends. I finally got to the point where I refused to suffer in silence. I realized that suffering in silence did not make me strong, it did not liberate me, it did not make me feel better, and it did not make anything easier to deal with. In fact, it had the opposite effect. I felt worse. As I began to express myself and tell people what was going on, I began to experience glimmers of peace and hope. I would tell people, no I'm not okay, today's not a good day, and I have physical pain, but here's what else is going on. Little things like that helped me conquer the psychological effects of infertility. I became okay with calling out for help. I surrounded myself with people who would help me.

I'm not saying the depression went away, but it got better. Being able to freely express my disappointment, anger, and sometimes self-hatred over how my body looked, helped me realize it is not me, this is the result of years of battling with reproductive issues.

Something else I had to stop thinking was that I would never have a normal life. That statement impacted how I viewed my life and magnified the sense of hopelessness, anxiety and wondering what was next. The paranoia magnified. I kept thinking the chronic illnesses were causing me to not have the life of a normal 20-, 30-, almost 40-something woman. I had to transition my thinking to focus on what was going on in my body, how to live with the symptoms of these illnesses and how to live with decisions I've made that, in the end, were best for me. It's not up to anyone else to decide what's best for my reproductive health — as long as I make decisions I'm at peace with, I will always be okay.

The diagnoses I received over the years dug up feelings of inferiority. I didn't realize how deeply things ran for me. There was a steep decline in my mental health, and I walked away from things and people I cared about, a career I truly love, and things I really enjoyed. I was consumed with managing the pain and paranoia, and the weight gain really made me feel insecure.

I remember there were a couple of times I was asked if I was pregnant or when I was due. First, let me say it is NEVER OKAY to ask a woman when she is due or if she is pregnant. Second, when someone is asked this question and she is not pregnant and may be dealing with reproductive issues, it can trigger something that could send her into a downward spiral. It is neither a compliment nor endearing. People really must learn that they do not always have to speak what they think.

It got to the point where I was so bloated and pregnant looking that the next few times (yes, this happened to me at least five times), I would just make up a due date or how many months along I was. It may sound silly, but it offered a little comic relief for me.

The reproductive system issues took over how I identified myself, they took over my thoughts, and my actions. I was emotional, very irritable, and lost interest in a lot of things. I no longer wanted to have a social life that revolved around planning for a potential accident; I wanted a normal life. But my normal was different than anyone else's. My normal was going to look different than the woman sitting next to me who has endometriosis, or the woman who has also had a lumpectomy, or the man who does everything he can to support and encourage his wife who is infertile. My journey is different, but the pain and the mental strain of being infertile was something we could all identify with in one way or another. Even if a woman is not deemed infertile, the weight of severe reproductive issues is something that connects us and causes us to look within and externally for ways to cope and heal.

A close friend of mine is a licensed mental health counselor, and one of her concentrations is postpartum depression. I thought it would be great for her to provide information on dealing with depression and emotional issues due to reproductive challenges, as the symptoms in these conditions are similar.

Meeting the Need: Self-Care is Not Selfish (Written by Taja Riley, M.A., LPC)

Importance of Mental Health Therapy

A therapist is a trained professional who assists children, adults, couples and families with a variety of life stressors like infertility and trauma. Working with a therapist is going to require you to work hard and dig deep. A therapist is going to challenge you and help you work through your feelings and emotions and change.

A therapist can help you clarify and achieve personal goals, work on communication skills, recover from past traumas, explore why past relationships have been destructive, work through depression or anxiety that affects your ability to function at home or work, survive a divorce or loss of a loved one, learn coping skills and resiliency, help your child with behavioral problems, reunite families, and more. Some benefits of going to therapy include helping you handle emotions from problems or stressors, helping you process things from the past that may still be affecting you, and assisting with issues affecting your relationship with a spouse or others.

Similarities between postpartum depression and infertility

Infertility is such an emotional rollercoaster that it can lead to depression in women. Giving birth is just the same, and often, both can result in feelings of sadness, worry and despair. It is not uncommon for women experiencing infertility or postpartum depression to feel inadequate, discontent and hopeless. Postpartum depression is a mix of physical, emotional, and behavioral changes that happen in a woman after giving birth. It can be caused from an array of different things, which include a chemical imbalance, lack of support, or sleep deprivation. Likewise, most women who have dealt with infertility will readily admit that they have spent countless hours being sad and have experienced periods of being emotionally overwhelmed.

A diagnosis of infertility and the ensuing treatment can bring a chronic state of stress, which can lead to depression or the existing feelings of sadness getting worse. Some research suggests that the emotional experience of women facing infertility is comparable to the emotional pain felt by women going through postpartum depression. Depression is more likely among women facing infertility if they have experienced it before receiving their diagnosis, have a family history of depression, or a lack of support, resulting in feelings of isolation. Infertility treatment and postpartum can be associated with extreme emotional changes.

Treatment options for women dealing with infertility, miscarriages or reproductive issues

Many women dealing with infertility or reproductive issues will initially try to find ways to cope on their own, or they will seek support from friends and family. There has also been a growing number of infertility support groups available, both online and in-person. Additionally, there are many mental health options available for women, including counseling, psychotherapy and relaxation techniques. For women who choose counseling, it can be short-term and help to increase coping strategies or provide help with making decisions as patients face many choices during treatment. Women who experience prolonged changes in their mood or sleep patterns or who have relationship problems should seek a more in-depth evaluation, as these may be signs of anxiety or depression.

For women seeking more long-term psychotherapy, specific therapeutic modalities may be useful. Studies have shown that narrative therapy, which helps women re-write their stories about infertility, interpersonal therapy, which focuses on improving relationships or resolving conflicts with others, and cognitive behavioral therapy, which identifies and tries to change unhealthy patterns of thought or behavior can be the most effective. All these treatment options can give relief to infertile women suffering from mild to moderate depression.

Psychotherapy can also be helpful for anxiety or depression, whether it is done individually, as couples, or in a group setting. For women who choose relaxation techniques, these can be extremely beneficial for dealing with high levels of stress due to infertility. Some of the options available to women and their partners include mindfulness meditation, deep breathing, guided imagery, and yoga.

I have always appreciated Taja's input and willingness to listen to me express myself and offer me advice on therapists to see.

In 2018, I accepted my normal, but was relentless in ensuring that, in spite of this new normal, I was going to get both the physical and mental attention I needed. I knew these reproductive issues meant making a decision I did not want to make. I knew that I needed help on various levels. In spite of wanting to, on several occasions, give up and stop trying to convince doctors of what was going on with me, I knew that I couldn't just throw in the towel. They needed to believe me. I didn't want to be a statistic of another black woman who was seriously injured, ill, or even died because of a misdiagnosis or doctors not taking seriously my symptoms and condition. I made sure I called my gynecologist, oncologist, and whatever other "ist" I had on my list to get the help I needed.

In retrospect, when everything began, I wish I would have sought the help of a mental health professional. I wish I would have sought out support groups in the different cities I lived in so I could have better coped with all the things I was thinking and feeling and dealing with. Not because misery loves company, but sometimes misery needs company to move from hopelessness to healing. It's okay to need help and support and I hope any woman dealing with infertility does not deal with it on her own. I hope that as women deal with the emotional, mental and physical impact of infertility and severe reproductive issues, they can — and do — seek help early and often. Get a regularly scheduled appointment with a mental health specialist and don't wait or allow the stigma of mental illness or imbalance to get in the way of getting the help you desperately need.

We are more than our diagnosis, and we can overcome our diagnosis by truly throwing ourselves at our healing. A lot of times our physical healing comes quicker when we feel good mentally, emotionally, and spiritually, so don't ever minimize what you're thinking and feeling as a way of saying, "It's just me." The truth is, it's not you at all. It's because of the reproductive illnesses you're fighting.

If you need therapy and you're unsure of where to turn, start with sites like TherapyforBlackGirls.com, PsychologyToday.com, GoodTherapy.org, and NAMI.org. You should also check with your medical insurance provider to get your list of service providers that fall within your healthcare plan. Utilize social media for support groups on Facebook. Get within a circle of people who can provide support at a level that is deeper than you going through the motions on your own.

❖ Spiritual Pain

In her book "The Broken Image," Tera Young eloquently explains identity.

> "When we think about the question, 'Who am I?' we must consider our identity and the makeup of everything about us. Identity consists of our physical traits, characteristics, strengths, abilities, weaknesses, passions, likes and dislikes. Some of our identity is based on life experiences and how they have affected us."

This was me. For a *very long time*, I struggled to figure out who I was. My life experiences really had me jaded, and I wasn't sure who I was beyond my life's difficulties. It was such a dark place for me. Tera went on to explain, "Many times, life experiences will often launch us into our purpose, because what we go through can make us stronger and develop a passion in us to help others who are experiencing the same thing," (p. 3).

I knew these struggles and victories, ups and downs, and mountains and valleys were for a greater good, but it was hard to see clearly through it all. There was such a deep hurt and grief that I was unable to truly consider how my situation would be a testimony to help others. I wanted the pain to end and couldn't understand what God was teaching me. Deep down, I wasn't even sure I fully trusted God. My mind and heart were disconnected from the truth; my mind said God is right here, but my heart was broken and uncertain if God was carrying me through or if He had left me to fend for myself. I was the sheep that was awaiting her shepherd to leave the 99 and rescue her.

For those that follow me on social media, I may look like a hypocrite because I post motivational and scriptural content even while questioning God and His plan for my life. In all honesty, my posts were a reflection of me trying to tap into Him and encourage myself. I was trying to reconnect my head and heart and trust God, even though I could not trace Him. These were my David moments (1 Samuel 30:6). This was me speaking the word of God to myself and being transparent about my humanity and emotions while searching for the answer to "why?" I was digging in, walking toward Jesus and making every effort to reach out to Him, touch the hem of his garment and be healed. I desperately wanted the feelings described in Psalm 28:7 (NASB), "The Lord is my strength and my shield; My heart trusts in Him, and I am helped; Therefore my heart exalts, And with my song I shall thank Him."

But the pain spoke more loudly than the hope and I continually asked, "God, where are you in the midst of this pain?"

I mentioned in talking about the physical pain and dealing with these reproductive issues, and ultimately issues that led to my infertility and subsequent hysterectomy in May 2018, that I found out precancerous cells had returned. It halted the writing of this book, caused me to take a step back. It also caused a deeper level of anger, uncertainty, and anguish within me. This occurred in early December 2018, when I awoke to intense itching, burning, and pain when I used the bathroom. I knew it was not a yeast infection — there was no odor. When I checked things out, all my skin had turned white again. Knowing what this was a sign of, I immediately called my oncologist and her nurse was able to get me an appointment for the upcoming Tuesday.

During that appointment, she told me I needed to have another operation; this one would be more invasive, due to my history with this condition. The healing process would be a little more painful than the last. I would have to be careful about my movements during the first week and would also be in more pain than usual. More pain than usual? I did not think it was possible, considering all I had been through already, but what did I know? Each new obstacle, each new mountain to climb, each new hurdle to leap over, each new challenge to face, presented something new to overcome. But mentally and emotionally, I really was not ready for it.

I remember calling my parents and telling them. At the time, my mom was out running errands, and I spent about 30 minutes on the phone with my dad, mostly in tears. There were moments of silence, moments of him not being able to say anything, and moments of him not being able to communicate his true feelings. I am pretty sure we were both feeling the same thing.

Growing up, we're often taught not to question God. Don't question God. Don't ask Him why. Just be thankful, because it could always be worse. But after 27 years of dealing with the same reproductive issues that had progressively become worse, I wanted to know why. I felt like God owed me the answer of why this was happening to me, and why it was going on for so long. Not even the woman with the issue of blood dealt with her issues for this long, so why was I still dealing with this and going through the uncertainty of praying that precancerous cells did not return, or even worse, fully mutate into a cancerous process? I was questioning God, and listening to my dad, and the pain and sorrow I felt intensified.

As a father, he had no idea how to help his child. He sat back and provided the comfort he could, knowing he could not take the pain away or explain why. All he had was his encouragement — and his faith. He told me I was the strongest person he had ever met, which made me smile because he is the strongest person *I've* ever met. He told me he wished he could take away all the pain and suffering because, at this point in my life, it seemed to be too much and he didn't understand why I continued to battle the same reproductive issues and why I couldn't have a "normal" life. But he expressed that he still had faith and that, even in the midst of his own health issues — the times he wanted to give up and throw in the towel — his family's love and faith kept him going.

And that's what he was able to give to me. Through his faith, he communicated to me that, while we don't understand what God is doing sometimes, and sometimes we don't understand why we have to keep going through certain things, if we give up, throw in the towel, stop pushing and stop advocating for our own health, we then succumb to the very issues we are fighting to overcome.

Succumbing was not an option. As desperate as I was sometimes for an answer and for an end to the pain and suffering, I knew that there was a way for me to proverbially touch the hem of Jesus's garment and get healing. I first had to understand that my healing would not always come the way I expected it, thought it should come, or what anyone else thought it should look like.

The end of our suffering does not always manifest itself the way we think it should. It doesn't always come the way someone in church tells us it will, because they may not be fully in tune with God's will for our lives and could be speaking out of high emotions, rather than truly hearing a word from God. That was very hard for me to accept, but I had to block people's emotionally-driven responses that were aimed at encouraging me. There were times people would say things to me that very easily could have made me upset or caused me to dwell on my situation. I had to train my mind to not think about what they said to me. I learned how to not react to what they said, but to simply offer a thank you and walk away or end the conversation. With every encounter, I had to remind myself not to have an emotional response.

I had to tune out certain people and operate in my own faith, my own beliefs, my own conversations with God and the things He revealed to me. If we are not careful of those from whom we receive "a word," we can be misguided into thinking, feeling, and believing that God is telling us to do something He is not. My focus had become strictly what God was saying and what was best for me. I could no longer listen to those who flung spiritual clichés without knowing the full story or really hearing from God to deliver a message to me. It took a while, but I'm grateful that I learned to discern who was speaking truthfully and faithfully and whose comments I should shake off like dirt from my shoes.

Then the Lord said to me, "The prophets are prophesying falsehood in My name. I have neither sent them nor commanded them nor spoken to them; they are prophesying to you a false vision, divination, futility and the deception of their own minds." - Jeremiah 14:14

God, I thank you for discernment and wisdom.

Using Faith and Focus to Move Forward and Finish the Process to Overcome the Pain and Convert it to Power

How would I move on from this? Bearing children was something society tells us makes women real women. Bearing children somehow solidifies your place in this superiority of womanhood — people always tell you that you know nothing about love until you give birth. But society lies. Society's rules are made up and should not be spread across demographics like peanut butter on bread.

The grief I felt was deep and gut-wrenching. Grief is unpredictable, strange, untimely, and sometimes lonely. I had to learn to feel everything and know that it is okay to grieve the loss of something I never got to experience and would not be able to now. I learned that my womanhood is not tied to my uterus and mothering someone is not tied to experiencing physical childbirth.

Through my journey, I went through the five stages of grief:

1. ***Denial*** - I could not believe what was happening to me. When it came time to have the hysterectomy, I wouldn't

accept it. I waited two years to have one because I refused to believe it was my final option for healing.

2. *Anger* - I was beyond mad. Why was God doing this to me? I was doing things the right way, wasn't I? I wasn't running around with a bunch of men. I wasn't trying to get pregnant by any guy I wanted. I wasn't living a risky life. Why was I being punished? There were so many women out there having kids they can't take care of or abusing their children, and there I was unable to conceive. Infertile. Barren. I was mad at God for this and did not want to hear that He had my best in mind.

3. *Bargaining* - I thought I could make a deal with God. "God if you just let me have one kid..." or "God if you just heal my body and give me the chance at being a mother..." I was hard at work playing "Let's Make a Deal." In my mind, God would allow me to have this desire of my heart if I were to give up something else.

4. *Depression* - I detailed this in the previous chapter, but depression plagued me for quite some time. I could not overcome my present situation and I felt an overwhelming sadness about my circumstance. I felt hopeless, and it seemed I would never be able to dig out of the hole.

5. ***Acceptance*** - As I mentioned before, I eventually accepted that I would not be able to have kids. I accepted the fact that I was dealing with a condition that may cause more severe issues if not properly treated. I accepted the fact that God had something else in store for me that involves being a mother in a different way than I planned for myself.

There were many conversations with my parents, brother and sister-in-law. Conversations with my best friends. Conversations with therapists. It was these conversations that helped me come out of the grief and help me convert my pain into power.

Through the grief process, through much prayer, through the emotional rollercoasters, and my desire to be healed, I learned how to convert my pain into power.

Here are the keys to convert your pain into personal power:

1. ***I became my greatest advocate***. One of the most painful experiences in dealing with infertility was having doctors at the beginning who did not believe me. They consistently tried to convince me what I felt was normal and that I needed to give it time.

   After years of listening to the advice of doctors, I changed my mind and began to listen to my body. I made calls, took photos of the blood clots for the doctors to see, would switch physicians and ultimately moved to seeing gynecologic oncologists who specialized in most of the conditions I learned I had. While I was tired, I refused to give up on the idea that I could be healthy again. I was my own greatest supporter and advocate and raised my voice the loudest to get the care I needed. I learned how to speak up for myself and, at times, became downright indignant when the doctors drug their feet on deciding on my care.

I researched dietary changes, various treatments, trends and other topics related to my conditions and went to the doctor with questions and a plan for myself. If at any time I felt the doctors were being lax about my treatment, I would ask why they were hesitant and have a conversation about what they felt was the best option. I was not afraid to switch doctors in order to find someone who would listen to me, believe me, provide the best care, and then check up on my progress.

2. *I began to see my healing differently*. Sometimes we want God to fix everything and make things the way we want them to be. In 2016, I began to look at my healing through a different lens — one that was deeply introspective. By 2018, I realized my healing was not going to be what I thought it should look like, and it probably shouldn't be. I took into consideration the necessity of a hysterectomy and, prior to that, the diagnosis that reproductive diseases

would more than likely make it difficult or impossible for me to conceive, and if I did conceive, I may not carry full term.

The way I thought about my healing began to hit me in a new way. Maybe this healing was to protect me from endangering my life, or the life of my unborn child. Maybe if I conceived and carried full term, the baby would have had birth defects, or worse. Rather than looking at the end as a curse, or punishment, or something being wrong with me, I began to see the end as a means to a new beginning: a healthy life and the ability to live freely and without the paranoia that plagued me for so long.

3. *I was not afraid to admit I wanted to give up sometimes.* I remember in 2018 when I was in church and felt intense pain all over my body. My blood pressure dropped, and my entire body was weakened to the point I could not walk or stand on my own. My dad had knelt down beside me, and I looked at him and said, "I'm tired." I felt tapped out. I wasn't sure my body was going to allow me to fight on and I wasn't sure I wanted to keep fighting. It was a scary moment for a fighter to not want to fight on, but it was my truth and I had to release it to get prayer and pull strength from other sources. I am far from being a weak-minded individual, but I wanted to be physically strong again.

4. *I stopped talking about my problems and began speaking about ways I could find solutions.* This was more for me personally. I was literally speaking things out loud, not just thinking about them. This really helped change my perspective on my conditions as well as my healing. In 2018, I fully understood and accepted my position to advocate for others dealing with similar issues. I saw my situation as an alert, a warning against typical medicinal practices, and a testimony that healing is different for each person. My approach was no longer about coping, it had become about finding solutions and ensuring I was able to support other women. I knew I needed to be a catalyst for positive change in how women see their healing and advocate for themselves.

5. *Faith. Focus. Forward. Finish.* This has been my personal slogan for a few years now. As I neared the day of my hysterectomy, and again in December 2018 when I was facing another operation to remove precancerous cells, I dove into my motto:

   a. Have *Faith* in God to work His will and guide me down the path that would strengthen me, heal me and help me become whole. It takes a tremendous amount of faith to live with chronic pain and go through each day believing your body will, at some point, stop betraying you. As I battled each day to overcome the pain, I prayed fervently that my faith, like Job, would be strengthened. God did that and so much more!

b. I had to learn to *Focus* on the positives and the idea that, as long as I was breathing, there was a chance to be made whole. If I felt pain, which was most of the time, I redirected my thoughts to acknowledge the pain, but find ways to move past it. Sometimes that was stretching, sometimes it was a hot shower, sometimes it meant scheduling a massage, but I focused my energy on converting bad feelings to positive thoughts and actions.

c. I moved *Forward* with doing what was best FOR ME. I stopped seeking advice or input and took steps to make decisions that would truly bring about positive changes in my life. I stopped thinking about why I should not do certain things and found the silver lining in how moving to one decision over another would be most beneficial.

d. I *Finished* the process of consideration. I finished the process of internal debate. I finished the suffering and pain. I finished the battle, and I made sure all things were done with my best interests in mind. The war over my body ended with me deciding that enough was enough and realizing I deserve a healthy life.

Every day, we are forced to deal with things that are not easy — and, no matter what you do, you're never truly prepared to handle infertility. Much of what I went through in dealing with reproductive illnesses and infertility was a means of me helping myself so that I could share my testimony and help others. I realized that, while it takes a great deal of courage to vulnerably share very personal pieces of your life, it is in those pieces that God can create a beautiful masterpiece.

We are our own greatest advocates, but sometimes we need someone to advocate for us until we find our way. I pray my story, this book and my life serve as that for others.

For any woman, any family, any man supporting a woman impacted by infertility, please know this: ***An infertile womb does not equate to infertile dreams!***

Bibliography

Young, T. *The Broken Image*. Get Write Publishing, 2017.